The Love That Moves the Sun and Other Stars

The Love That Moves the Sun and Other Stars

David Russell Mosley

Foreword by Matthew A. Rothaus Moser

RESOURCE *Publications* · Eugene, Oregon

THE LOVE THAT MOVES THE SUN AND OTHER STARS

Resource Publications
An Imprint of Wipf and Stock Publishers
199 W. 8th Ave., Suite 3
Eugene, OR 97401

www.wipfandstock.com

PAPERBACK ISBN: 978-1-6667-8066-6
HARDCOVER ISBN: 978-1-6667-8067-3
EBOOK ISBN: 978-1-6667-8068-0

07/27/23

All quotations from the *Inferno* come from Dante, *Inferno*. Translated by Robert and Jean Hollander. New York: Anchor Books, 2002. All quotations from the *Purgatorio* come from Dante, *Purgatorio*. Translated by Robert and Jean Hollander. New York: Anchor Books, 2003. All quotations from the *Paradiso* come from Dante, *Paradiso*. Translated by Robert and Jean Hollander. New York: Anchor Books, 2007.

To my mother, Ruth Ann Mosley, who entered the
next stage of her journey on September 3, 2022.

Thank you for always believing in me and encouraging
me to write. May eternal light shine on you, always.

To all those who have supported my writing,
most especially my loving wife, thank you.

Contents

PURGATORIO

PARADISO

Forward

THE DIVINE COMEDY, WRITTEN by Dante Alighieri (1265–1321), is the great poem of Christianity. It tells the story of Dante the Pilgrim's journey through the three realms of the afterlife–hell, purgatory, and heaven–on his way to behold God face-to-face in the beatific vision. We first meet the Pilgrim when he is lost in a dark wood, stuck in a state of spiritual misery. But he is rescued from this state and taken on a journey in which he will learn about God, himself, and the world. Guided first by the Roman poet Vergil and then by his own poetic love Beatrice, the Pilgrim's journey is a salvific one in which he learns about the true nature of virtue and vice, salvation and damnation, and the divine mystery of justice and love. The poem itself is made up of three *cantica*, each based on one of the realms of the afterlife: *Inferno*, *Purgatorio*, and *Paradiso*. These are then divided into cantos, or songs, totaling 100–the number of divine fulfillment and perfection. It is in the hundredth canto, at the point of poetic fulfillment, that the Pilgrim achieves the spiritual perfection of beholding the trinitarian face of God in the beatific vision. It is in this visionary moment that Dante names God as "the Love that moves the sun and the other stars" (*Paradiso* 33.145).

The *Comedy* is not only the most celebrated Christian poem, it is also recognized as one of the "great books" of world literature. But what makes it great? Surely its greatness is due to its genius, its literary and intellectual accomplishments, its poetic bravado, and its moral seriousness. But its greatness also lies in its generativity, its ability to draw others into its poetic and religious imagination, its invitation to readers to join the Pilgrim on their own journey to God. Like the souls that Dante meets in heaven who proclaim about him, "Oh, here is one who will increase our loves!" (*Paradiso*

5.105), the poem invites readers to share in its truth and beauty, to add to and to increase the love it hymns.

The volume of poems that you hold in your hands is just such a response to the *Comedy's* invitation. David Russell Mosley's lyrics are a testimony to the ongoing power of Dante's verse. In each of these 100 poems, Mosley joins Dante on the journey to the vision of God. In the spirit of the Poet, he invites his readers to join him. Mosley writes in the first- person, highlighting how we can all make Dante's journey our own. And this indeed seems like one of Dante's goals in the *Divine Comedy*: to move *us* from the dark wood to the heights of heaven.

I think the most fruitful way of reading the present collection of poems is together with the *Comedy* itself. Read a canto from the *Comedy* and then read the corresponding poem from Mosley's collection. This is analogous to the call and response of Christian liturgy. Reading Mosley's poems in direct response to one of Dante's cantos is a way of meditating on that canto, entering into the spirituality of the *Comedy*.

But the present collection is more than a meditative commentary on Dante's poem. It undertakes its own journey, through verse, toward God. Mosley writes truthfully and passionately about both the beauties and difficulties of the contemplative journey of spiritual transformation, of moving ever deeper into the heart of wonder that fuels prayer and worship. There is in these poems a vibrant and urgent love for God, but also a candid openness about the struggle of attuning ourselves to grace, of aligning our wills with God's will, in whom is our peace (*Paradiso* 3.85).

In this way, Mosley's poems most remind me of *Paradiso*. They are not striving after perfect description or mimesis, trying to capture the truth of God in language. Instead, they are aimed at making the divine reality of Love present to us. And so these poems not only allow us to see and understand Dante's *Comedy* in new ways. They also invite us to become Pilgrims ourselves, to set our feet on the road that ends at the goal of all of our lives: to be moved by the same Love that moves the sun and the other stars.

—Dr. Matthew Rothaus Moser

Preface

I FIRST BECAME ACQUAINTED with Dante's *Divine Comedy* as I was writing my PhD. I had already read C.S. Lewis's *The Discarded Image* and was familiar with the medieval worldview, but reading Dante allowed me to enter that world. Ever since then I have read the complete *Divine Comedy* nearly every year. For the past 5 years I've even taught it to high school students. Dante has been the subject of my teaching, my research, and my writing for well over a decade now. So when I was casting my mind about for a new poetic project, doing something with Dante's most important work seemed obvious.

The book you now hold in your hands is 100 poems, each reflecting on some aspect of every canto of the *Divine Comedy*. I try to represent not only Dante's perspective, but my own. So when we reach Limbo or the Wood of the Suicides in the seventh circle of Hell, I do not let the medieval perspective have the last word. Still, Dante was an incredible theologian in his own right and so his work warrants this kind of response.

Readers need not fear, however. If you have not read the *Divine Comedy* these poems will still, I pray, mean something to you. Dante's own work focuses on issues of sin, repentance, corruption, and salvation. In my poems, I try to do the same. I pray that these poems may even inspire readers to pick up, whether for the first or the hundredth time, Dante's work and read it for its own merit.

The title of this book comes from the final line in the *Paradiso*, the final part of his *Divine Comedy*. Each section, usually called canticles, ends with the word stars. For Dante, the stars and all other moving bodies, are representatives of Christ's all redeeming Light, refracted throughout the cosmos, showing us different aspects of God's nature. So too, each of my sections ends with the word stars and plays with this understanding that meaning of the planets to medieval minds can still convey something to us.

I pray that as you take up these poems you will join me as I have joined the pilgrim of Dante's story. Together we will journey to the depths of sin through the purgation of repentance and to the all-consuming vision of God.

Inferno

"Midway in the journey of our life I came to myself in a dark wood, for the straight way was lost."

—*INFERNO* 1.1–3

"Abandon hope, you who enter here."

—*INFERNO* 3.9

"'One may not be absolved without repentance, nor repent and with to sin concurrently—a simple contradiction not allowed.'"

—*INFERNO* 27.118–20

"Then we came forth to see again the stars."

—*INFERNO* 34.139

"The Dark Wood"

Inferno Canto 1

And I have also lost the mountain path
And fallen in the forest dark and grim,
Enduring what so often feels like wrath

But is just Love that's boiling over the brim.
Falling off the Mountain of Delight,
The Sun still rising and not yet growing dim,

My sinner's eyes are blinded by its Light.
So I must find another path to tread,
A path of hellish darkness and of fright,

Yet one that will bring life back to the dead.

"The Savage Way"

Inferno Canto 2

A coward's yellow-belly now runs across
The middle point of my most sinful self.
How can the savage way be more than loss,

Loss of all the causes of my health?
Where are the holy tears they shed for me,
The Jewels up on Heaven's highest shelf?

As they descend from Heaven's purity,
Raining down their just and holy prayer
I feel the hope of what I'm meant to be,

But first I must traverse the wicked stair.

"Abandon Hope"

Inferno Canto 3

What hope is there as I pass the gate of sin?
Where in the unmoored clock of starless sky,
This unholy marsh, this wretched refuse bin

Will my final place be set before my eye?
Will I be kept from either Hell or Heaven,
Lukewarm and living without eternal tie?

Or will I cross the swamp with sinful brethren,
Descending down to find purgative tears?
I've risen by the work of wicked leaven,

And must descend in spite of all my fears.

"Limbo"

Inferno Canto 4

Are pagan philosophers and poets trapped,
Suspended with their unfulfilled desires,
Caught in a cage whose monstrous mouth has snapped

Shut, and leaving them outside the fires
Of punishment or discipline that grows
The soul to a place where it will never tire.

If Socrates cannot reach the Celestial Rose,
I lose what little hope that I had left.
Unless to deeper truths Dante's eye was closed

And Primal Love will not leave us bereft.

"Venus Infernal"

Inferno Canto 5

I am enthralled by the movement of desire.
The tail encircles twice to show my place,
And I must join the murmuration in fire.

Now look upon these sinners, see the face
Of Venus Infernal, of Reason losing the reigns
That guide the soul-chariot's horses from place to place.

But being in my body, I will regain
A chance to leave the "Lovers" to their lust.
Yet first I must wake so I can be moved again

By the diurnal power of the Just.

"Hungering"

Inferno Canto 6

Wakened by the hungry growls of a dog,
I see the worm condemned to eat the dust.
Ravenous it growls, its talons flog

The sinners known to us as gluttonous.
He snarls and slobbers over their wicked souls,
Infernal tri-part beast, old Cerberus.

If only I could hunger for my goal,
Hungering for justice and the right,
The way these sinners hungered for their bowl,

I would not need this journey in the night.

"Lady Fortune"

Inferno Canto 7

Wheeling round and passing back and forth,
The order of my loves is out of sync
While apathy and anger find their worth.

Lady Fortune's wheel will rise and sink,
Taking me to unseen heights and depths,
While I am written out in pen and ink,

My sins exposed in their expansive breadth.
Sullen sighs set the brackish marsh to boil,
And to find a way across I am inept.

Will I find my way beneath the soil?

"The City of Dis"

Inferno Canto 8

Disordered passions to disordered will
Give way, and for a moment I take pleasure
In the tearing down of sins that kill.

I approach the iron city of evil measure
Where rebel angels mock my wandering soul.
But I must pass them by to find my treasure,

And Reason cannot get me to my goal.
To pass through Dis, I'll need angelic aid
And the grace of God before I make so bold

To see the lower levels my sin has made.

"Medusa"

Inferno Canto 9

My sins will make a statue of me yet,
As I tremble waiting for the wrath of Love.
Encircling serpents gather and beget

In me division from the truth above.
Entombed in fire, divorced from what is real
I turn away from all that I should love.

Only the will of God calls me to heal,
But I must turn my sight from sin and listen
To the voices that only wish me well.

Further I must go from the stars that glisten.

"Hope Rekindled"
Inferno Canto 10

Passing through the city of fire, I fear
That I might also cut myself off from you,
Removing myself from all that you hold dear.

Meanwhile, the damned can tell me partial truth
About the worldly end to which I'll come.
But I must wait for one with better view,

One whose eyes will finally see me home.
But who is the one, the one for whom I wait,
My patron voyager who calls out welcome?

She'll only appear when I reach my fate.

"Heresy"

Inferno Canto 11

Even those who sit in Peter's chair
Are not safeguarded from the threats of Hell.
So what of me who breathes the lower air?

How can I keep from heresy, please tell
Me, one who travels now the dangerous path.
But before I have an answer, I hear a yell.

The violent have made murder of their wrath.
Against their God, creation, and each other
They rage and rage. In their infernal math

They add only wrongs, and by them are they smothered.

"Phlegethon"
Inferno Canto 12

Phlegethon, that river filled with blood,
Boils over with my bestial rage,
Boils over into an angry flood.

The equine half-men gallop across the stage,
And kill me with their grapples and their bows.
But I am brought to life by the turn of the page.

My hatred of my brother is like an arrow
Shot to strike him dead right where he stands.
So I must put it down and come to know

The Love that overcomes and understands.

"Entreeing"

Inferno Canto 13

I'm lost again, but in a different wood,
Stuck amongst the brambles and the thorns.
New thoughts creep in that life is not so good.

They say these thoughts will lead my will to scorn
The gift of my most precious life and being.
And yet, these thoughts like talons leave me torn.

My will has been diminished, no longer seeing
How to resist these foreign, invasive thoughts.
Can I even assent to my entreeing

When my will is replaced with a different crop?

"Blasphemy"

Inferno Canto 14

The violence done myself I leave behind
And turn to all the ways I try to harm
My God, through that first sin, the sin of pride.

What's wicked in me tries to make me warm
By making me the ruler of my life,
Thinking I can change the world by a charm.

But I will be impaled by my own knife
If I put myself in a higher place.
Being my own god leaves only strife

And my violence leads me to disgrace.

"Love's Wrath"
Inferno Canto 15

There are those who've left the natural path,
Burned down to their souls with lustful fire
So now they run or burn in Love's full wrath.

If I do not want to suffer in this mire,
Then I must live within sweet Nature's bounds
Or else my life becomes my funeral pyre.

The One who set the planets in their rounds
Is Author of the drama we call life,
So I mustn't follow Folly out of bounds,

But rather take the Lady Wisdom for my wife.

"Remember"

Inferno Canto 16

Why do my sins call out, "Remember me"?
Why do the damned long for temporal fame,
When hope has been cast out beyond the sea?

But when on the proper path these subtle flames
Are snuffed out when I think of them too long,
And now my cord is used for a different game.

Before my face appears a bestial one,
Who leads me down into a deeper violence.
We cannot stop the song of the eternal Sun

But we can make a mockery of its silence.

"Usury"

Inferno Canto 17

Now woe to those who make a game of art
By only making money, nothing more.
To create from nothing is not our part,

Nor should we leave our neighbors bereft and poor.
And when we gamble with another's work,
We harm them for a truly paltry score.

And yet we must pay or else they'll go berserk,
Calling for our lives, a pound of flesh.
So pay up now and do not dare to shirk,

For wickedness will one day meet his Justice.

"Flattery"

Inferno Canto 18

The iron castle mocks the true Mansion
Of God, where lies can have no part or home.
Here flattery would see me as one who stands in

The shit that filled my mouth at heartless welcomes.
And to manipulate a woman for
My own seductive pleasures will become

A terror of torments that leave me ripped and sore,
Tortured by the sons of the father of lies.
Still if I can leave these tortured pores

I will find my hope in star-filled skies.

"Simony"

Inferno Canto 19

"Come and let me buy the Holy Spirit,"
So said the patron of these burning sinners,
But now they pay the price and with fire bear it

On their heels, for they thought themselves the winners,
But the offices of the Church cannot be bought.
They saw themselves as spiders, as the spinners

Of webs in which their prizes would be caught.
But Satan caught them in their webs instead,
The Just upends the fraud that their hearts sought.

And yet, could they still consecrate the bread?

"Divining Pride"

Inferno Canto 20

The Lord makes fools of fortune tellers and turns
The deceits they wrought in life back on themselves
Like a false fire that lights but does not burn.

These liars claimed to work some mighty spells.
They claimed the stars did more than just incline
And showed as proof the books upon their shelves.

To claim a knowledge that belongs to the Divine
Is to claim certain kind of pride
And I too have claimed that what is his is mine,

So I must be humbled by the coming tide.

"Political Aspirations"

Inferno Canto 21

The bridges of Hell are fallen, broken down,
For Christ has already defeated death by death,
But evil still appears just like a clown

Or like a politician who in one breath
Will smile and tell you yes when he's been paid
To Change it to a no. And like the rest

My reason leads me to believe, afraid
To look more clearly at their evil smiles,
That my debt to them can go unpaid.

And yet they wait to tear me all the while.

"Skinned and Flayed"

Inferno Canto 22

Evil will always drag evil down
And here the captors also are the damned.
Sin cannot do anything but drown.

Vice can never come up with a plan
To overcome some other vicious thought.
All I can do is run and not just stand,

For I must run or else I will be caught,
Torn and dragged beneath the boiling pitch,
Skinned and flayed, dismembered by my thoughts.

But first I must climb out of this dismal ditch.

"Hypocrisy"
Inferno Canto 23

O Let me not be found a hypocrite,
One whose smile says yes but heart says no,
So I will not be nailed down and found unfit,

Trampled over by those who slowly go
About their way in clothes that look like gold,
But are lead no philosopher could undo.

I lay upon the ground like a carpet sold,
Sold to clean the shit off sinners' feet.
But I can still repent and be made whole,

If I fall upon your mercy seat.

"The Weight of Sin"

Inferno Canto 24

As I travel further into sin,
Seeing all the ways it causes death,
I pause before I can go further in.

I stop to rest myself, to catch my breath
Before I see the new and twisted horrors.
Like a phoenix rising from its death

I rise, standing firmly on the floor.
Sin has weighed me down, but still I go,
Seeking grace on some far distant shore,

Stealing back my life from Hell below.

"Stolen Nature"

Inferno Canto 25

A brood of vipers hide in wait for me,
Seeking to steal what little hope I've left,
But now they writhe as they turn out to be

Snakes in the grass, of human nature bereft.
Transformed into the creatures they pretended
To be in life, with fingers long and deft.

But will my sins also leave me upended,
Returned to a beast to wallow on the ground?
For I have abandoned what I should have defended

And have stolen fear to hide inside my wound.

"False Counselors"
Inferno Canto 26

Sailing out to follow other stars,
To leave behind the true and wisest council,
Will lead myself and others to fiery bars,

To prison when there isn't even an ounce still
Left inside of the truth. Deceit
Is not the way to fight or lead or council,

But can lead to a life, a life replete
With lies proclaimed as truth behind closed doors,
A life that's filled with violence and conceit,

And can lead to death outside forbidden shores.

"False Repentance"
Inferno Canto 27

Can a man repent before his sin,
Can a penitent's life be so unmade
That after death they're sought by angels grim?

Time is like a children's game that's played
From beginning to middle and back to beginning again
And I must convert again or else be made

A devil's plaything, with nothing left to gain,
Nor even anything that's left to lose
Besides, perhaps, some temporary disdain.

Which path I'll follow is only mine to choose.

"Rend Yourself"

Inferno Canto 28

Prepare to rend yourselves and not your clothes
If what you scatter is not seed but men,
For you will join the torn, the rent, all those

Who cut the branches, removed them from the stem,
Who cast them out to shrivel up and die
And sowed a deathly pallor on their end.

But before I see what's in my brother's eye
I must be sure to look inside my own,
To see if I have caused myself to die

Cut off and turned away from the Eternal Throne.

"Alchemy"

Inferno Canto 29

"I can turn all that is base to gold!
"And give you wealth you'd never hope to gain,"
So claimed the errant philosophers of old.

Whether this could happen is never made plain,
But if it were it would not be a sin.
Rather the lie lies in their deceitful game.

Yet I have also made light of the dim,
Pretending that this lead is truly precious,
This lead of mine, this darkness and the grim

Reality that lies are so infectious.

"Counterfeit"

Inferno Canto 30

Distended by retention of my evil,
I thirst for Truth which I have left behind,
But cannot drink, and so I must leave full

Of evil nothings blowing in the wind.
Counterfeit, I am no longer I,
Instead a mockery is left to unwind

And bare itself to the eternal eye.
But I can be returned to my true form
By looking up to the all-consuming sky

Which can press me into a holy kind of charm.

"Babel"

Inferno Canto 31

Titanic fear can only make me pause
As I descend into the final hole.
Tangled language leaves me with a clause

I must accept, confused, gigantic, whole:
"Raphel maì amìcche zabì almi."
The words become confused inside my soul.

Pride and treason lead to this psaltry
Plucked by my nimrodic, treacherous fingers.
I make it play the holy, holy, holies

But about myself and so my sin still lingers.

"Pride"

Inferno Canto 32

There is a bottom to the universe,
A point that's furthest from the Celestial Rose.
The sin that lies within this icy hearse

Is punished in me by my tears so frozen
To my eyes and face I cannot cry,
Cannot repent of that which made me lose

All hope and any chance of seeing the sky,
But my blood can still flow warm in me,
And Grace can warm the tears stuck in my eye

So there is still a chance I can be free.

"Treason"

Inferno Canto 33

The ice of pride now gnaws me from the inside,
And blinded by my sin, I stumbling enter
And kick the head that comes up from the root side

Like a cabbage rotting in the winter.
Decay is slowed by the infernal ice,
And so a kick from me causes leaves to splinter,

And opens up what once was closed like a vice.
I hear a tale of woe from this talking head,
Thinking that his story would suffice

To trade his treason for the holy bread.

"The Beast Restrained"

Inferno Canto 34

Cast down to occupy the furthest point,
The Traitor flails his hairy legs in the air.
His place in Hell can only disappoint

Those who hope to find him ruling there.
Infernal seraphim, a parody,
Whose treason cannot now come to repair,

He sought to overthrow the Trinity,
But my descent has found him in icy bars.
Descending, I ascend to newfound clarity,

To southern shores that shine with different stars.

Purgatorio

"I turned to the right and, fixing my attention
On the other pole, I saw four stars
Not seen but by those first on earth."

—*PURGATORIO* 1.22–24

"When such great splendor overwhelmed my sight
Greater than any I had seen before,
That I was dazed by its unfamiliar brightness"

—*PURGATORIO* 15.8–12

"'I have brought you here with intellect and skill.
From now on take pleasure as your guide.
You are free of the steep way, free of the narrow."

—*PURGATORIO* 27.130–32

"The Antipodes"

Purgatorio Canto 1

Rising up, I find a different way
With many different stars that shine to guide me,
So bind me with the reed and wash my face.

Like Venus, I ascend out of the sea,
Ready to be rid of that hellish hollow,
Ready to find the Love I could not see.

This is the path of Love that I must follow,
The mountain path that will at last leave me purged,
So I may ascend still higher like a swallow

Following that divine and holy urge.

"The Journey Begins Again"
Purgatorio Canto 2

It is the Morning of the Resurrection
When the nails of iron Mars are broken down
And I begin to sing with new inflection.

But in Splendor's Light, I still must drown,
Even when the Light is just reflected,
And so I cast my eyes upon the ground.

I may be moving on, but am still infected,
And should not pause, but start upon my way,
Because my wickedness must still be inspected.

I ascend while the Sun is rising on this day.

"The Mountain"

Purgatorio Canto 3

Seeking for a way to climb the mountain,
This giant rock which will serve as my foundation
For the day on which I'll drink from the eternal fountain,

I pause to ponder the hope of my salvation.
A shadow obscures what I had once thought clear.
Can dying breaths remove me from damnation?

Can I be cleansed by crying holy tears?
I've wandered off and must again find my way,
Moved by Love and Justice, not by fear,

And climb as Light still shines upon this day.

"Penance"

Purgatorio Canto 4

A glimpse of hope returns just as the Sun
Climbs to its zenith, but from the West, not East,
Showing me the War might well be won.

But to ascend to the eternal feast,
I must see my path rise at a different angle,
And feel my heart beat penance in my breast.

My knot of sins must be untied, untangled,
For I have let my loves become disordered.
I ask for prayers, my beggar's cup still jangles

As I approach the gate that leads to order.

"Late Repentance"

Purgatorio Canto 5

What if I waited to the last to repent,
My final prayer a solitary word?
Could I have hope that I'd be heaven sent?

Could I have hope that I would still be heard?
Is this kind of prayer a way to find
The path that leads to the Eternal Word?

How can I keep from sinking beneath the rind
When with whom I've lived I've hurt and scorned?
Will they think of me, bring me to mind

And pray for one who caused them so much harm?

"Prayers for the Dead"
Purgatorio Canto 6

Can the prayers of those on earth still help
The souls of those who have gone on before,
The dead who flounder now just like a welp,

Helpless and hopeless until their Mother who bore
Them descends and lifts them up with care?
Perhaps this is the opening of the door,

Perhaps our Mother Church will fill the air
With cries for her children who did at least repent
And so these cries ascend to God as prayer

Calling on the One whom Heaven sent.

"Night on the Mountain"

Purgatorio Canto 7

The Sun is setting and with it takes away
All sight of mountain paths that lead me home.
And so I wait until another day

Can shine upon my road to bid me welcome.
So until then I'll watch the exalted cast
Down before the Lowly. For beyond the dome,

The dome that's filled with shining stars at last,
Sits the Woman to whom they all must sing,
The Woman by whose yes now brings repast

To those who call upon her Son as King.

"The Serpent Slain"

Purgatorio Canto 8

It can be easy to forget who won
All those years ago on calvary
When I am still left waiting like someone

Who has been promised to be at last set free,
But must still wait and work in the meantime.
And so I wait and am not surprised to see

The evil serpent as up the mountain it climbs,
But now it comes unto a different end.
For Christ has come, both human and divine

And what was split apart, he came to mend.

"St. Lucy"

Purgatorio Canto 9

In a dream I feel myself ascend,
Ravished by the Love of God most high,
Carried closer to my final end

By one who carries in her hands her eyes.
I need her light to find the three-fold steps,
And to see what lies beyond the day I die.

The gate unlocked will lead to repentance's depths
And how to cure the seven deadly sins
And follow the way which only grace directs.

The waiting's done and so I must step in.

"Humility"

Purgatorio Canto 10

In statues that seem to move and speak, I see
Examples from before the holy birth,
Examples of the great humility.

David dancing naked, knowing the worth,
Understanding his simple place in the world
No king or emperor can ever search

And reach the virtue of that lowly girl
Who changed the Cosmos by simply saying yes.
But I am doubled over, a branch that's furled

By a weight that repentance makes weigh less.

"Pride Discovered"

Purgatorio Canto 11

These eyes that thought that they could look to heaven,
Could place myself among the shining stars,
Could rise to divinity by my own leaven

Are now cast down, no longer looking far
Beyond my humble station in this life.
I must retrain my sight, undo this scar

And yet I cannot change by my own might.
I need the love that sends celestial winds,
The Love that moves all things away from strife.

I'm humbled now so soon I can ascend.

"Pride Destroyed"

Purgatorio Canto 12

Casting down my eyes still filled with pride,
Training them to see a different way,
I see below my feet an image wide

And set with those who've died and now must pay
The wages of the sin in which they lived.
Repentant, I must turn and face the day,

And in the Light and wind, I will be shriven.
My pride put down by blessed humility,
By God's grace this virtue is now given

And by its Light, he gives me more to see.

"Envy"

Purgatorio Canto 13

The grace of God is in me and unsinning,
But there are many sins still left to purge.
I raise my eyes as in a new beginning

But first they must be shut to a different urge.
My heart and eyes would only have complained,
"The wine is out!" would be my only dirge.

Though cleansed of pride, my eyes are not unstained,
And I must learn of generosity.
Iron wire sews them shut, retains
Them to see the other in Charity.

"Sin Exposed"

Purgatorio Canto 14

If only I could hide my sinful source,
Put it away where no one could ever find,
But the Sun above has set a different course,

And one day soon, will send a different wind
To blow away the chaff and useless straw.
So until then, I must be a different kind

Of man, and must not go against the Law,
The Law that makes me the keeper of my brother,
It turns my heart of stone to flesh without flaw

Which hears the celestial call of my true Mother.

"Caritas"

Purgatorio Canto 15

Love that is hoarded is always becoming less,
But Love that's shared must always so increase.
It gives the Lover more with which to bless.

Thus envy is by Charity decreased
Until it dies and Love can take its place.
But there are other sins I still must cease.

A Mother's love can scold without disgrace;
A Father can show strength when his meek,
For in the sin of wrath we are displaced,

Pretending to be strong when we are weak.

"Free Will"

Purgatorio Canto 16

The Heavens may incline but not determine
The way in which my body and soul may go,
Giving space provided for me to discern in

Which way my will will lead me or else follow
The buffets of the winds that always change.
But no outside cause can lead me down below.

I must choose, must will for the exchange
Whereby I lose all sight of Heaven's glory.
No wrath can blow this smoke away, no rage

Can lead me to the Lamb of ancient story.

"Wrath"

Purgatorio Canto 17

Leaving behind the smoke that reins in wrath,
I leave behind the love that pulls things down.
Love of my own "greatness" creates a path

To envy's river, where, if I don't drown,
Or seek a way to climb out of the mire,
Then to wrath's perverted shores I'm flown.

But now I'm moved away from hate-filled ire,
Away from love devoid of so much good
That to look for it would leave me tired,

And find too little love for the understood.

"Sloth"

Purgatorio Canto 18

Just like the bee who has the sweet desire
To fill its waxen combs with running honey,
So I am lit within by Love's pure fire.

And yet, my will can make it dark for me,
By inattention to my nature's call.
For I can pursue power and fame and money,

I can even know the Good, the True and all
The works and virtues I am called to live,
But if I do not respond, or if I fall

Short, then sloth is all I have to give.

"Greed"

Purgatorio Canto 19

With zeal I ought to run from excessive love,
And yet I find my face down in the dirt.
Not content to see the stars above

I grasped the empty goods that made me hurt.
When roving eyes do not glance up to heaven,
But listen to the siren, then their dessert . . .

No! I must repent and find that safer haven,
Even if my lust for wealth will leave me
Seeing first the worthlessness of earthen

Goods compared to that celestial sea.

"Generosity"

Purgatorio Canto 20

I see the cure for my unwieldy greed
Is not in spurning all that God made good,
But in generosity, I'm freed.

My loves cannot be ordered by my mood.
Nothing that is so changeable as feelings
Can serve as source for our renewing food.

No. We must be like Christ who sent us reeling
When he said that we must eat his flesh
And drink his blood and so be in his keeping,

Giving ourselves to Christ, we are enmeshed.

"Prodigal"

Purgatorio Canto 21

What songs will angels sing when I am ready?
And will I hear the heavenly spheres rejoice?
Will the earth beneath out feet become unsteady

When at last I sing with God-willed voice,
All glory to our Lord above the spheres?
On that day I'll make the righteous choice,

To will one thing, which is purity I hear.
But until then, I must continue on,
To seek the Lord's forgiveness as though far but near.

Though prodigal, I'll be welcomed like a son.

"The Way, the Truth, and the Life"

Purgatorio Canto 22

There are many paths to Christ for those
Who have the eyes to see, and look to find
The Truth. For anyone who will but choose

To seek the Truth will find it in any kind
Of song or story told by any teller.
The Spirit always whispers in the Wind

And blows the Truth into every home and cellar.
But to listen is not always to hear
And Christ can be put off altogether.

So I must seek him out despite my fear.

"Gluttony and Temperance"
Purgatorio Canto 23

With skin that's sallow, drawn, and scabbed, and starved,
I must learn to hunger and thirst aright.
Enchanted streams and trees just like those carved

In my memory of Eden bright
Give off a scent so sweet unto my nose
That though I cannot taste I am made Light

For they have taught me how to smell the Rose
And how to long for only what is Just.
I no longer long to choose different than I chose

But now I long to be raised up from the dust.

"Gratefulness"

Purgatorio Canto 24

How can a little fruit cause so much trouble?
How can my appetite lead me astray?
This tree produces fruit just as a bubble

Produces joy in children while at play.
It's plentiful, why can't I take a bite?
Why can't I listen to what the snake will say?

Because I know to eat it isn't right,
I can't mistreat the things that God has made,
And food must be received with different sight.

It is a gift and with thanks it is repaid.

"Venus Purged"
Purgatorio Canto 25

Preparing to be purged of all my lust,
I stop to contemplate this thing called man.
How do we grow, how do we learn the just

And ordered means by which our bodies can
Grow and be infused with an immortal soul?
How does it happen, according to what plan?

All answers must be partial and thus not whole,
And yet we know we are designed by Love.
In Love we're made, and it's our final goal,

But first there's still the fire up above.

"The Refiner's Fire"

Purgatorio Canto 26

Poets seem to gather near the fire
Which will refine them all as glistering gold,
But poetry can lead to unbridled desire

Whether it is my path or another it unfolds.
The closer something is to the Divine,
The more we try to buy what isn't sold,

The more we'll think our God a lower sign,
Confuse him with the fire that burns my heart,
And not as the Fire that will my heart refine.

Enough of talking, I must make my final start.

"Purgation"

Purgatorio Canto 27

I feel the fire of God's love burn brighter
As the scales of sin come crackling off.
And now undragoned I feel myself full, lighter

With levity I now can turn my thoughts
To beauty won through nature or through act.
With pleasure as my guide I must be off.

For I can nearly contemplate the facts,
Can see the forms that give their shape to things
Embraced by God in his covenantal pact,

Forgiven and shrieved, I hear the rivers sing.

"The Forest of Forgetting and Remembering"

Purgatorio Canto 28

And now I find myself in another wood—
Always to begin and never end—
But here the ancient trees will bring me good,

Not like the forest, dark, in which I went
Groping and grasping as though I had been made blind
But now I find a forest for God's friends,

A place to refresh, to seek, to seek and find
The rivers ready for my final bath
To wash away my sin, to wash and bind

My feet onto this last, celestial path.

"The Holy Dance"

Purgatorio Canto 29

So many visions dance before my eyes:
Seven gifts brought by the Holy Spirit,
Two dozen elders, the first to glimpse the prize,

Four beasts escort the one, who, if we can hear it
Is God and man, while seven ladies dance
And four men walk behind the chariot.

I see no sword, no spear, no pointed lance,
No arms of war in the face of Love so ardent.
How is it I have come to have this chance,

This glimpse of the Holy Bride who comes triumphant?

"Faith and Reason"

Purgatorio Canto 30

Philosophy and reason leave me now,
I am bereft of my once trusty crutch.
Limping forward, I must learn somehow

To see the highest beauty, not to clutch
To those perversions to which I have succumbed.
Sorrow must become for me as much

As were my sins which gave me so false a welcome.
From my eyes must rain the holy tears
Before these sins can finally be undone.

And so I contemplate and they appear.

"Lethe"

Purgatorio Canto 31

Now bathe me in the waters to forget,
Not that I sinned, but that it had control.
The memory of sin can still beget

A shame that leaves repentance only partial.
But this is not why memory was made,
So we could be like pigs so hot we wallow

In the mud of sin and be afraid.
Looking deeper in, I find the eyes
That re-membered me out of dust and clay.

Looking into them I see the skies.

"The Tares amongst the Wheat"

Purgatorio Canto 32

Before I saw New Adam and his Bride,
And they redeemed the home we long have lost.
But now I see the Wife from a different side.

We've commingled with the world and it has cost
Not gold or gems, but Christ's consuming perfection.
Tear out the tares, but then the wheat is lost.

The Church may seem so full of vile corruption
And we may want to leave it to its pain,
But the gates of Hell can never bring destruction,

And God's gifts will always, always remain.

"Eunoë"

Purgatorio Canto 33

Euonë's waters lap upon my feet,
And like a tree awaking I must drink.
These waters wake in me a power that greets

The Morning Light that shoots through Night's black ink
And brings with it the joyous Morning Song.
I drink so deeply, not afraid to sink

That I am soaked from root to bough before long.
This liquid light, it does not burn, it chars.
It awakens life, its greening power is strong.

I know my branches will dance among the stars.

Paradiso

"The glory of Him who moves all things
Pervades the universe and shines
In one part more and in another less."

—*PARADISO* 1.1–3

"'Just as long as the festival of Paradise
Shall last, that is how long our love
Shall dress us in this radiance"

—*PARADISO* 14.37–39

"Here my exalted vision lost its power.
But now my will and my desire, like wheels revolving
With an even motion, were turning with
The Love that moves the sun and all the other stars."

—*PARADISO* 33.143–45

"The Celestial Heavens"

Paradiso Canto 1

All things enjoy a kindly inclination
To return to their true source and home,
And I can journey home with Christ's salvation.

O True Sun, you burn away the gloom,
And by your Light you draw me further in
And further up, into and beyond the dome,

The spheres that radiate your Light and spin.
It was my will that drew me down to nothing,
My will that kept me trapped inside my sin,

But turn my will to you and I rise to being.

"The Music of the Spheres"

Paradiso Canto 2

Beyond the fire that encircles the earth
The Heavens burn with a different kind of Light.
The stars declare its glory to be worth

All praise and honor given in the night
As angels dance and music we can't hear
Radiates in colors beyond our sight.

We cannot sense the music of the spheres,
The sweetness at the back of the universe.
Through thick and thin it calms us and it cheers,

But no instrument of man can sing its verse.

"Lunacy"

Paradiso Canto 3

What does it mean to wander, to turn away?
And what if my will is not wholly in it?
Can I be entirely to blame?

They thought the moon was perfect in its movements,
Receiving and reflecting the Holy Light
And yet its change made it seem inconstant.

Perhaps somehow, to wander can be right
Or at least its not a sin if it is wrong,
And will to will transformed to something bright.

And this will be the bliss for which we long.

"The Mansions"
Paradiso Canto 4

I pray my will will always seek return,
Not to the star from whence my soul was born
But to the heart of fire for which I yearn.

The stardust in my body was still-born
Created by the Uncreated One
Clothed in a soul, but I must still be warned

That there are many mansions in his Kingdom.
The stars incline, but cannot force my will.
I alone can choose what must be done.

And by the grace of God I'll have my fill

"Mercurial"

Paradiso Canto 5

Perfect Love will cast out imperfect sight,
And so I'm overwhelmed at the spark of Love
Who called me, not to vows of wrong and right,

But to the yes and no of God above.
So as I say another, willing, yes,
I meet the Lord of Language, of honor proved.

And here, I'm filled with an increasing bliss
Where friendship grows and grows only greater
Because the more we love, Love does not grow less,

But more and more it shines increasing favor.

"Holy Fame"

Paradiso Canto 6

There is a kind of hope that seeks to live
In the memories of those who will outlast you.
It seeks to be remembered and to give

Honor, fame, and glory to all those who
Fight for faith, to bring about the Kingdom.
But eternal fame is won by only a few

And to seek it is to be a bell's ring done
Before the hammer even leaves its side
Tolling once, once and then forgotten.

How wonderful this is not counted pride!

"Good Friday"

Paradiso Canto 7

Eternal Beauty brought us that Good Friday,
Where God-in-flesh took on the fitting pain
That was our due to give for all the ways

We let our will run loose, unchecked, untamed.
He could have overcome this sin in us
In many ways to help us to regain

A life made good, a life made just.
But he chose a descent that we could not endure
So we might learn the Path out of the dust

And in his Life, we are made divine and pure.

"Venus Paradisal"

Paradiso Canto 8

The Heaven of Love shows to me all God's order,
How the circling of the cosmos leads to life
Set by Providence before the world or

Light itself had shown us man and wife.
The circling of the Heavens still declares
And whittles out all nature with a knife.

But our souls descend by heavenly stairs
Giving us the freedom of yes and no,
For God desires order but also cares

That loving is to choose and so to know.

"The Lover"

Paradiso Canto 9

To be a lover is to be like the One
Who set the stars to swirl in Cosmic Dance,
For He loved the world and sent to it his Son,

To give the world its one and only chance.
But those who loved another thing too much,
Must sink below the earth or be enhanced

And raised to the third heaven. No matter what
These whores and fiends all sought to love at first,
They found and then delighted in the just,

For those who rightly drink will rightly thirst.

"Wisdom's Light"

Paradiso Canto 10

There is an Eye that watches over all,
Casting light wherever it deigns to look.
And in that eye there is a ring, a ball,

A circle of the sacred ones who took
The time, the chance, to study you, o God,
And read the cosmos, because it is a book.

These, the Lovers of Wisdom, Lovers of God
Inspired my own attempts to live and see
The face of him who made us, Christ our God,

In the high and low, in Man and tree.

"Rays of Truth"

Paradiso Canto 11

Now in the Eye all wisdom is found to be one,
And old rivalries will come together
As they find their way into the Sun.

Wisdom always bears the fruit of her Lover,
Just as the Sun makes full the earthen womb
And in the sphere of the Sun they live forever

Spreading the truth of the Man come from the tomb.
The lengthening of days will bring new life.
Without our help, reform will die too soon,

And wait for a wanderer to make her his wife.

"True Alchemy"

Paradiso Canto 12

The fruit is left out to ripen in the Sun
So long as it is dressed, is dressed and kept
By one who loves the faith and does not run

When the work is hard or he feels inept.
We ought to till and work for the Lord of Gardens,
Sowing seeds and knowing to accept

The harvest as a race that is hard won.
But soon the Lord is to coming to his home,
And we will see the true Sun's light starred in

His eyes when he declares the harvest is done.

"The End of Wisdom"

Paradiso Canto 13

What is wisdom without an end in mind?
A sailor setting out to find nothing,
A pilgrim who has yet to pick a shrine.

And what of wisdom found in a humble king
Who seeks to know only how to rule
And does not seek to know eternal things?

And what about the hasty, unwise fool,
The well-intentioned ignoramus who
Thinks his stone or rock a precious jewel?

Only in Christ the King is Wisdom true.

"A Bodily Feast"

Paradiso Canto 14

How often we forget the good of bodies,
The matter in which we're made in which we die.
We treat it like a sort of spiritual hobby,

And think it will end like so much pie in the sky.
But Paradise is filled with festal lights
Meant for spirit and a physical eye.

We'll feast as though there is no longer night
Because the God from God became a man,
Defeating Death through meekness not through might,

And so became our feast, our festal lamb.

"Martial Martyrs"

Paradiso Canto 15

What does it mean to find a martyred root
From which I come, a lowly hanging branch,
One that will not trip me, catch my foot,

But bears me up, and takes for me the lance
That would send me straight to Hell,
But sends them on to the celestial dance?

And what if I have no one who lived so well,
Who bears the martyr's crown upon their head,
Whose prayers can help me come to dwell

With those who've died and are no longer dead?

"The Warrior Redeemed"
Paradiso Canto 16

Between the Baptist and the god of war
I think again of my own ancestry.
I need no smile, shining like a star

To warn against some pride in family.
The only blood that's pure is Jesus Christ's,
And he's a son of ignobility.

An adulterous king, a murderer, by rights
A man whose vicious name should be forgotten,
This man, this sinner, his brightest ancestral light.

And yet repentance lets us be brought in.

"White Martyrdom"

Paradiso Canto 17

Exile makes you a certain kind of martyr.
White, not red, for you get to keep your blood,
But not your home, so find a different quarter.

A party of one, removed from former good,
You have to find a different way to live,
To live your life as something understood,

A prayer that leads you on, that makes you give
Your art and life up as a holy gift,
A gift of penance, a gift one who's shriven,

A gift to people whose prayers you will uplift.

"Evil Gatekeepers"

Paradiso Canto 18

Just as we call that solemn Friday Good,
So now I move from death to breathless joy,
Singing in the ether about the blood

Of Love and Justice spent for us to enjoy
The abundant life our God has made us for,
But which we once abandoned like a toy.

Yet still there are some hidden at our core
Who seek to lead my simple soul astray,
Denying entry through the eternal door,

Forgetting that our Lord is the only way.

"The True Gate"
Paradiso Canto 19

Who will and will not find the joys of heaven
Is not a choice to be made by mortal man,
But woe to those who think they are the leaven

And yet deny true Justice again and again.
Christ is truly the one and only gate,
And it's from him that we receive amends,

For he's the one who took our sinful weight,
He's the one who opened up the door,
So woe to those who deny us bread to eat

Who keep us from the wine that freely pours.

"Prayer"

Paradiso Canto 20

You let us conquer you to conquer us.
Your providence includes our acts of will,
And though we may not understand, it's just.

A divine trap, consuming you, we will
Find ourselves consumed by you, our food,
And thus we enter death that does not kill.

A jovial judge, you've come to do us good,
To rescue even those we cannot guess,
To bring us Love, a love that knows no mood,

But stays constant, and makes an enemy a guest.

"Providence and Fate"
Paradiso Canto 21

The flaming soul descends the starry ladder,
Arriving in the time that God ordained
For me to contemplate the holy pattern

Of smileless faces and of music contained
Within the deafening sounds of celestial silence.
Despite the height, my senses all remain

Mortal, transfixed, suspended, not by chance
But by the plan of God that men call fate
And from His view is called "My Providence"

Where no amount of time can find me late.

"Holy Eyes"

Paradiso Canto 22

While still within the World, within the wheels
Of time, my eyes cannot perceive the deep
Truth that hides behind the World and feels

More real than even the ground beneath my feet.
But soon I will see all the Truth unveiled
When I ascend beyond this mortal keep.

Until then do not let me be curtailed,
But let me learn to measure out the prize
So when I come I may at last avail

Myself of the sight of Truth with holy eyes.

"The Light of the Cosmos"
Paradiso Canto 23

Among the stars there reigns another Sun
Against whose Light there is no chance or defense.
For from this Light all other lights have come.

My eyes are overwhelmed, I lose all sense
Until my mind reforms into itself,
And now I see without the slightest wince.

Within a Rose, I see the truest Self,
Which gathered to it the Lilies of the field,
Which is the source and summit of all wealth.

And from its Light, you will not find a shield.

"Faith"

Paradiso Canto 24

This is the most precious gem that I can find.
Its substance made of unseen certainty;
It proves the existence of the Holy Wind.

The virtues find their home in its quiddity,
And I have learned it from the Old and New.
The poets told us all their prophecies

While the Lilies showed us them come true.
And from these stories a miracle was born,
People believed them and found in them their due.

And so this is the faith that I have learned.

"Hope"

Paradiso Canto 25

We have been made for a certain end,
An end declared in all of holy writ.
God made me, made you to be his friend.

Expect the Glory that his grace, and your merit—
Itself a gift that's given from on high—
Will grant you life, though now you cannot bear it.

Beyond this hope, another virtue lies,
One that makes us sons of a different kind,
Yet bound to kindness. A light then strikes my eyes,

And once again, this Light has made me blind.

"Love"

Paradiso Canto 26

My first father did not comprehend
The virtue that once left me without sight.
He turned away and made himself his end.

Now as I'm no longer overcome by Light,
But can perceive it in a truer form,
The language that would let me say it right

Is gone, is gone, no longer keeping warm
The hearts of men made from the lowly dust.
And yet, our languages may at last perform,

And speak the Love that is right and just.

"True Reality"

Paradiso Canto 27

Greed and simony are not as real,
Nor any other sin that catches man,
As where I stand, a drunkard in a wheel

That has no place, no where that our minds can
Comprehend. The moving place that moves
All other spheres. And like a wind up man

Is moved by gears, so this is moved above,
Moved by desire in the mind of God,
And moving by our Lord's consuming love.

The First Moved is spun by the Love of God.

"The Cosmos Inverted"
Paradiso Canto 28

With eyes of Love, I see the universe
Inverted now from what I once believed,
While it still moves in a dance that's been rehearsed.

The inner and outer are not as I've conceived.
My journey outward is really a journey in.
What I thought was the center I now perceive

Is furthest out, the beginning point of sin.
And God does not reside in an outer ring,
But is the Source and Summit of all that spins.

And whirling round him saints and angels sing.

"The Nine Choirs"

Paradiso Canto 29

The angels, agents of the highest Love,
Were made but not for anything It lacked,
But to represent what is above,

And move the potencies toward their final act.
To every atom they serve as ministers.
To celestial and terrestrial life they act

As guides and guardians, not finishers,
But as many colors of refracted Light,
They point away from all things sinister

Toward the True Source, and to the end of night.

"The True Center of All of Things"
Paradiso Canto 30

Beyond beyond and yet the inner inmost
Is where our God can be said to dwell.
Beauty here will rise up to the most

Splendid sight no eyes can see so well
As those made whole in the first and final sphere
Where Light flows like a river in a swell.

And if I could turn a redeemed and wholesome ear
From this final Light would sound a song,
One greater than the Music of the Spheres,

A Music that will overcome all wrongs.

"The Celestial Rose"

Paradiso Canto 31

At the center of all things I see a rose,
Where all the good I've seen truly resides.
Seated here I see another Rose,

The Queen of Heaven who since her assumption abides,
Ever looking on the threefold Light.
Despite her prominence, no hint of pride

Can be read in her face so shining bright
That nothing held within it could be hidden.
Around her all the other created lights

Come to see the One by whom they're bidden.

"Empty Seats"
Paradiso Canto 32

In the rose I find there are empty seats.
The Queen of Heaven's court is not yet full.
This absence does not signify defeat,

There are no holy knights who have been pulled
Down to death, but rather all these chairs
Are waiting anxiously to be made whole.

Just as in the beginning days came in pairs,
The formless being formed but not yet filled,
Until the forms were formed with all his care,

So now these chairs will wait till all is fulfilled.

"The Love that Moves the Sun and Other Stars"
Paradiso Canto 33

With the prayers of my Queen and Mother,
My eyes look up to the only existent One,
Who through himself made me son and brother.

This Light is Love and brighter than any sun.
It wheels so smoothly I can see that there are three,
And yet these three are bound, an eternal One.

And in one Light, I see our human nature,
One Light, divine and human, bearing scars,
In Him I see the last, our final adventure,

The Love that moves the sun and other stars.